facebooking CRAZE

for Internet Marketers

Table of Contents

Introduction: Why Use FaceBook? 4

How to Register Your FaceBook Account 6

How to Write an Attractive Profile 8

Adding Friends and Building Your Network 11

How to Get More than 500 Friends in 30 Days 13

How to Get Targeted Prospects from FaceBook Advertisements 15

How to Start a Group and Do Joint Ventures 19

Some No-No's on FaceBook 22

The FaceBook Frenzy: To Join or Not to Join? 24

Introduction: Why Use FaceBook?

In marketing circles, there is a great deal of talk about FaceBook. FaceBook is a social networking site that came quietly into the Internet scene in early 2004, when it was founded by Mark Zuckerberg. Mr. Zuckerberg was still a student at Harvard University at that time, and FaceBook was geared towards college students only.

Within the FaceBook interface, users are able to create their own profile, complete with personal data, professional data, and a picture. They are then able to add other users of Facebook to their circle of friends. They can add people they know or request to add complete strangers, therefore widening their network, or circle of friends.

Friends – or strangers soon to be friends – can be located with their email address, by region or city, by profession, by their school, or numerous other options. Once a person has joined your circle of friends, you can interact with them by sending them messages or leaving notes on their profile, which is essentially called 'writing on one's wall.'

As stated, FaceBook was initially designed for use by college students – first those attending Harvard, and later those attending other ivy league schools. A lot has changed in four years, and now anyone over the age of 13 can open a free account at FaceBook and start interacting with others. Today, there are more than 80 million people using FaceBook.

Since FaceBook has become open to non-college students, some of the most famous Internet Marketers, including John Reese, Mike Filsaime, and Willie Crawford have found that the social networking site is more than just a way to connect with old friends and to meet new friends, it can also be used as a valuable marketing tool.

Internet Marketers around the world have found that FaceBook allows them to interact with people on a more personal level, which in turn builds even greater trust and stronger relationships with customers and potential customers. It has even been said that social networking, especially through a site such as FaceBook, is more effective than marketing to one's opt-in list in many ways.

FaceBook is no longer a 'little known secret.' It's been blown wide open, and it is essential that you start using it and including social networking in your Internet Marketing endeavors – just as the most influential Internet Marketers are already doing.

How To Register Your FaceBook Account

We've all had those experiences where signing up for a service – especially a free service – turns into a nightmare at the worst, or a headache at the least. You typically have to wade through questions that have little to do with the service you are signing up for, and of course view countless offers in which you have no interest.

This is not something that you will encounter when you sign up for a free account at FaceBook. The entire process takes five to ten minutes, and few questions are asked. In fact, the only questions that are asked are those that are absolutely necessary for opening an account. It's definitely a refreshing change, and here are the steps that you need to take to get started with your own free FaceBook account:

1. Go to www.facebook.com

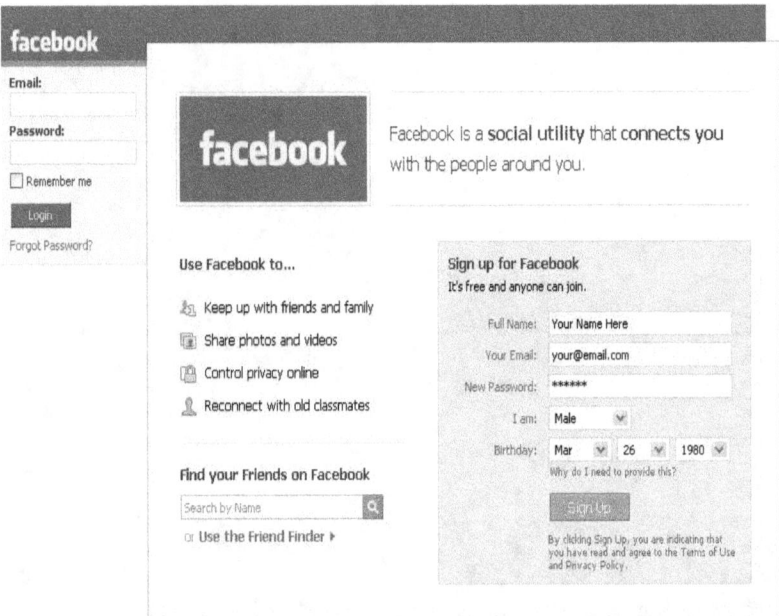

2. In the box where it says to 'Sign up for a free account', enter your name, email address, and password. Select whether you are male or female, and fill in your date of birth. You must use your full name here. This will not be shown on your profile. You must also enter your date of birth, so that FaceBook can ensure that you are over the age of 13.

3. Go to your email and open the confirmation email from Facebook. You must click the link in the email to confirm your account or you will not be able to activate your Facebok account.

4. Once you've clicked the link in the confirmation email, you are good to go. You can login to FaceBook, start setting up your profile and add friends to your list. There is a utility you can use to search your address book to see if any of your current friends are a member of Facebook.

That's all there is to setting up your free FaceBook account. The entire process takes less than ten minutes, although setting up your profile will most likely take longer. The signup process, however is very easy and mostly self explanatory and it is just a matter of reading what information is being requested and filling that information into the incredibly short form to get started.

How to Write an Attractive Profile

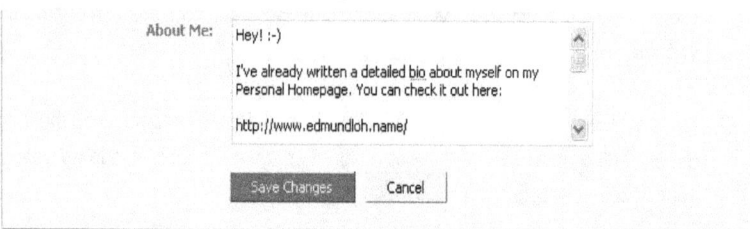

Now that you are all signed up and confirmed as a FaceBook user, you need to set up your profile. This is quite easy to do but it does require some thoughts. Because you are using FaceBook to increase business and to connect with customers and business associates, it is essential that you use good business sense when setting up your FaceBook profile.

Obviously, when filling in the blanks, you fill with care. For your screenname, as a business person, the best thing you can do is use your own name. Many people use their business name and if you want to do this, you might want to consider setting up a second account with your business name, then connect it to your personal FaceBook account where you are using your real name.

People generaly don't want to see 'the business.' Instead, they want to see the face behind the business – you.

With each blank that you fill in, remember that potential customers, current customers, and business associates will be reading what you've written. It cannot be said enough – write with caution. You want to sound human and friendly but you don't want to go overboard here. If anything else, answer questions in a way that gives you more credibility in your market.

While you may not see the extra applications that you can add to your FaceBook profile in the beginning, it won't take long before people start sending you applications for you to add. Again, use caution.

Since you are using your FaceBook account for business purposes, you do not want to clutter your page up with a bunch of silly applications that have no connection with your business. Furthermore, each application you add slows down the load time of your page and too many can also cost your credibility to decrease, which is something you definitely don't want.

When it comes to adding pictures, make sure you upload your professional photo. You may add photos that are more 'casual' as well, so that readers can see that you really are human and that you really do have a life.

Finally, make sure that you include the website addresses for your business. But for your main URL, use the one that links to a page on your website where people can get more information about you, your experience, and other information that makes you an expert in your field.

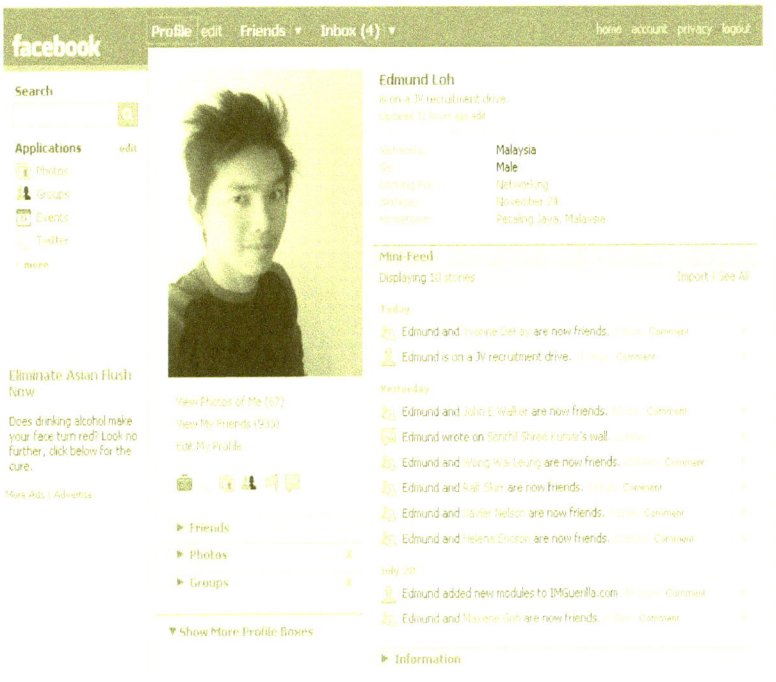

When you are finished, have a few other people review your profile for you. Check it for spelling and grammar errors. You might even consider comparing it to the profiles of other successful Internet Marketers just to be sure that you are on target – at the same time, however, make sure that it is unique.

Adding Friends and Building Your Network

There is nothing worse than logging into your FaceBook account, clicking on your friends list, and seeing the words 'you have no friends.' That's an assault to ones sense of self confidence and self worth! You've got to start adding friends as quickly as possible.

Start with the people that you already know. You want to get that friends list populated fast. You can use the FaceBook feature that will search your email accounts at Gmail (http://www.gmail.com), Hotmail (http://www.msn.com), and AOL (http://www.aol.com).

If it discovers some of your contacts are Facebook users, it will give you the option to send those people a friends request.

From there, consider other social networking sites that you belong to and the friends that you have there – even if they are not in your email address book. Check to see if they have an account on FaceBook. Write a message in NotePad so that you can copy and paste. It should be very short and to the point.

You may need a couple of different messages. One might say "I know you from such and such forum or social networking site and I would like to add you to my friends list here at FaceBook." Another might say "I realize that you do not know me personally, but I see that we have xxx in common, so I would like to add you to my circle of friends."

Look for people that you know from other social networking sites, social bookmarking sites, microblogging (Twitter, at http://www.twitter.com), forums, and even blogs that you commonly read, as well as people who read your blog. Also consider adding other Internet Marketers, including marketers who are in the same niche that you are in.

From there, you can use the search features to find people in your general area as well as people who have interests that are in common to yours. Just add them even if you've never had any contact with those people in any other online or offline venue. Look at the friends of your friends. This is an excellent way to grow your network as well – the thing that you have in common is the original friend.

Just remember that every person you add to your network is a potential customer, a customer, or a business associate, and you definitely want your network to grow as large as possible, as quickly as possible to get the most benefit from FaceBook.

How to Get More than 500 Friends in 30 Days

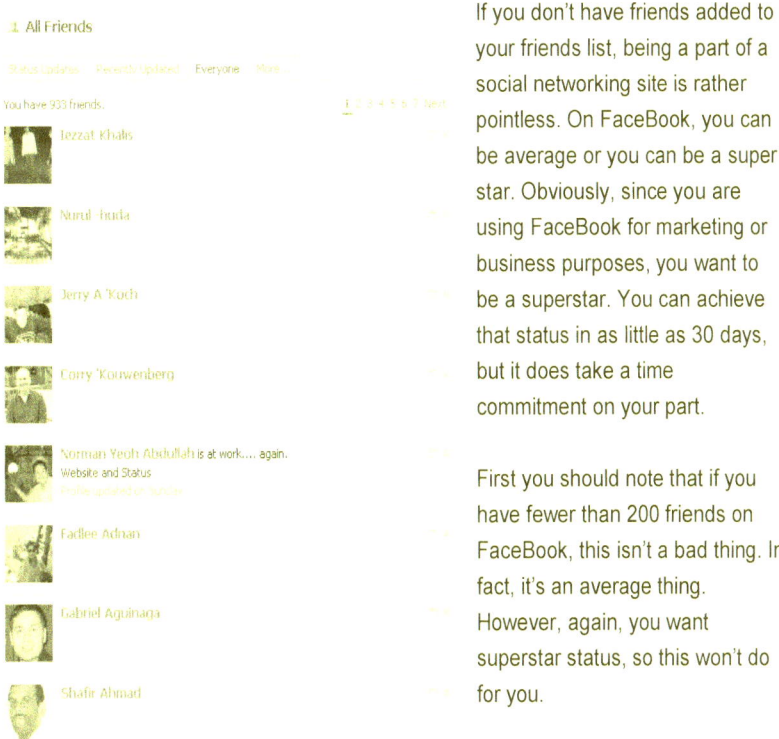

If you don't have friends added to your friends list, being a part of a social networking site is rather pointless. On FaceBook, you can be average or you can be a super star. Obviously, since you are using FaceBook for marketing or business purposes, you want to be a superstar. You can achieve that status in as little as 30 days, but it does take a time commitment on your part.

First you should note that if you have fewer than 200 friends on FaceBook, this isn't a bad thing. In fact, it's an average thing. However, again, you want superstar status, so this won't do for you.

Once you have 500 friends, you are considered to be popular, and people will gravitate to you, and when you have between 800 and 1000 friends, you're essentially a FaceBook celebrity. Eventually, that's what you should be working towards, but for now, let's concentrate on becoming popular, with 500 friends.

Do not use automated software that adds friends to your FaceBook friends list. This defeats the purpose of social networking. Instead, do it the 'hard way'. You will come to realize that the hard way really isn't hard at all.

The first thing to do is to join all of the Internet Marketing groups that you can find. There are plenty of them out there. Each time you join a group, send a friend request to all members of that group.

Not all members will accept the request, but the majority of them will. This can be a little time consuming, but it is well worth the effort in the end. This should easily net you 200 to 300 friends. Try to add at least 30 new friends each day, for the full 30 days.

Once you've exhausted the IM groups, find other groups that are related to your business. For example, if you are in the personal development group, find those personal development groups, and start adding members as friends.

Use your existing website to get more friends, as well as your blog. Post your FaceBook badge on your website and blog. Make a blog post and invite your readers to add you as a friend on Facebook. If you twitter, tell your followers to add you on FaceBook. If you have a mailing list, send out a note and invite them to join you on FaceBook.

Again, it does take a concentrated effort on your part, but it is well worth it in the end, and if you are dedicated, you absolutely will have more than 500 friends in less than 30 days, and if you want that superstar celebrity status at FaceBook, you can continue to add new friends for an additional 30 days to reach that goal.

How to Get Targeted Prospects from FaceBook Advertisements

FaceBook allows you to not only connect and find new friends and associates, it also allows you to promote your business through various types of FaceBook advertisements. These are not free advertisements, however it is very affordable.

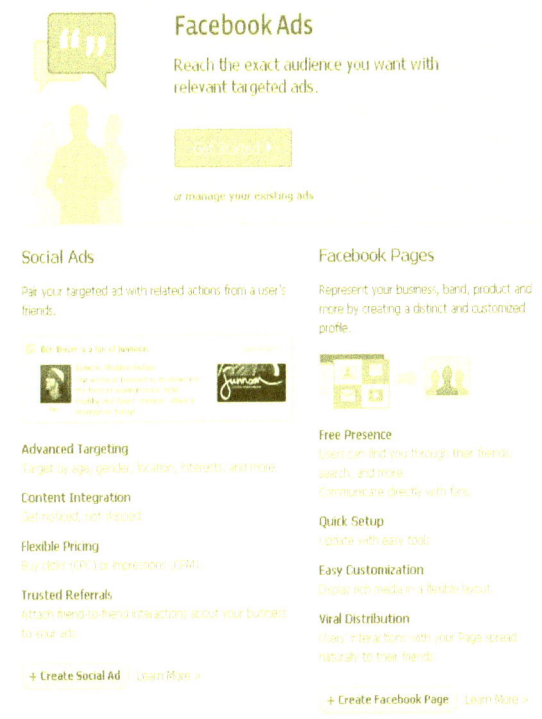

First, there are two options when it comes to how you pay for the advertising. You can purchase clicks, which is known as CPC advertising, or buy impressions, which is known as CPM advertising. Most advertisers will likely choose CPC, since this means that the advertisement attracted the prospect enough that they actually clicked on the advertisement. With CPM, you can't even really be sure that your advertisement are noticed.

One of the nice things about advertising on FaceBook, however, is that the ads can be highly targeted to your desired audience – by gender, age, interests, location, and many other variables. If you don't believe this, just login to your own profile, and on the left hand side of the page, under your navigation links, look at the advertisement there. The chances are very good that it relates to you in some way.

You can also elect to have your advertisement integrated with the content on FaceBook as well, which means that your ads are included in the News Feeds and social stories on FaceBook, as they relate to that content, and they appear in the content so naturally, that it isn't even obvious that it is advertising.

Use the Trusted Referrals feature when you set up your advertising. This means that advertising will be shown to your friends, based on the actions that they took while they were visiting your profile, and this isn't limited to just your friends. It can also show advertisements to friends of friends.

There are those who have not gotten good results from FaceBook advertising, but this is often simply because they are not targeting the right audience. It may take a bit of trial and error to get the results you want, but when you find the right ad, for the right market, the results are astounding.

Building Credibility with FaceBook

It takes more than setting up a nice profile page and adding friends to truly build your credibility with FaceBook. There are other things that you need to do on the site that will let your profile visitors know that you do indeed have credibility and you are in fact trustworthy.

Start by adding the testimonial application to your profile page. This application can be found at http://www.facebook.com/applications/Testimonials/2588290420. Your friends will use it to create testimonials about you, which will appear on your profile. You can also import testimonials that are sent to you via email, or used on your website. Just make sure that your testimonials are from real people – and put the testimonials from other FaceBook users first.

Next, encourage your friends to write on your wall. Here, you must use caution. There will always be those friends who want to advertise on your wall, and you must discourage this – preferably without offending your friends who are doing that advertising.

When they attempt this, send them a nice note and tell them that you don't want any advertising on your wall, but that they are free to write on your wall otherwise. The best way to get people to write on your wall is to write on theirs – and do not advertise when you do so!

You want a bunch of people writing on your wall – as long as they are not advertising. You could even run contests among your network, which involves writing on your wall. For example, who has the most creative post, or who can post the most to your wall in one week? Make sure that you impose rules concerning the wall writing content when you announce the contest. The purpose for doing this is to raise the number of posts on your wall – as this raises your credibility.

When you set up your profile, make sure that you use a professional photo. Also make sure that you throw in some casual photos as well, to really put a human face on your profile. Do not forgo the professional photo in favor of casual photos, however. It's also a great idea to include photos related to your work.

For example, pictures of you at the latest seminar or past seminars, pictures of you in casual settings with other marketeers, pictures of you working, and things of this nature are great.

Always try to see your profile from a prospective customers or joint venture partners point of view. What are they seeing? What is the content saying to them about your credibility. Also, view other successful marketers profiles and really pay attention to how they make their credibility shine through with their profile.

How to Start a Group and Do Joint Ventures

One of the most important Internet Marketing related features on FaceBook is groups. This goes far beyond joining groups to find new contacts. It also includes creating groups of your own for the purpose of joint venturing – even if that joint venturing won't take place until a future date.

First, let's examine how to set up a group. The process is extremely easy. Simply log in to your account then click on 'groups' in the navigation panel on the left. At the top of the next page, you will see a button that says 'Create a New Group'. Click that button, and fill out the form. It's just that simple and can be done in a matter of minutes.

The hard part is determining what type of group that you want to start. What is the groups focus? All groups must have a focus otherwise, they are essentially worthless.

Let's say that the focus of your group is to joint venture with other Internet Marketers, but you aren't sure exactly what type of joint venturing you want to do at this point – or how you could work with the potential members in the group for the purpose of joint venturing. In this case, you may want to start a mastermind group for Internet Marketers. This is very broad and it leaves joint venture possibilities wide open.

Now, you must consider who you want to be in your mastermind group, so that you can send out invitations. Mastermind groups are typically small – usually just ten to twenty people, so this shouldn't be very hard. However, you must remember that you will eventually want to joint venture with these people in your group. Therefore, you want to be very selective with your invitations.

Think about joint venturing – outside of social networking. You obviously need someone who has products or the necessary skills to create quality products. You need someone who is great at copywriting. You may need a web designer. You obviously want people who have large opt-in lists, and/or large networks of people.

You definitely want people who are active on FaceBook. You will invite people from your own circle of friends in most cases, but you can invite people who have the interests and skills that you require, who are not currently your friends as well, simply by searching for them from within the group interface and inviting them to join.

The next obstacle is to get your group active and to get the members participating. Ask questions that require input from members. Offer information that you know the members will find useful.

Start showing them what you are made of and what you have to offer so that when the opportunity or need for a joint venture comes up, they know what you can bring to the table. At the same time, pay attention so that you know what they can bring to the table as well.

Make sure that all content that is being provided to the group is useful, valuable information. Don't advertise to your group and don't allow other members to advertise either.

Let information flow naturally and freely without the advertising. You will find that you and other group members are easily able to work your products and services into the conversations or articles that are being published to the group – as those products and services relate to the information.

Finally, if you are a bit unsure about how to operate a group or how to make it a highly effective group, consider joining another small group that is already set up and being operated by someone else. You must really pay attention to how the members interact with each other and the content that is delivered through the group. This will definitely give you some great ideas for your own group on FaceBook.

Some No-No's on FaceBook

While you are building your credibility on FaceBook, there are certain things that you could do – easily – that will completely undo everything you've accomplished to date and prevent you from ever building credibility through this social networking site in the future – plus it can happen in a matter of minutes.

Here are some things that you definitely want to avoid doing on FaceBook:

1. **Do not spam people's inboxes or walls.** This will not only cause you to lose credibility, it can also cause you to get banned from FaceBook. FaceBook is one of the best social networking sites in existence and it is important to keep it in it's currently clean, spam free state, so that it remains a useful and valuable tool for everyone who uses it.

2. **Never post messages on other people's walls with the sole intention of linking to your own website.** It's obvious and just makes you look desperate and greedy. Don't link anywhere at all. Instead, post interesting comments and people will click your name to learn more about you from your profile, where you should obviously link to your websites.

3. **While you want to give yourself and your business a human face, you really don't want to get overly personal** – especially with photos and videos. You aren't searching for a hot date – you are trying to build business credibility. Don't forget that – ever.

4. **Don't add an abundance of silly applications to your profile.** It just clutters your profile, makes it load slow and really just takes the viewers attention away from that which you want their attention firmly glued to – information about you and your business.

5. **Never have 'cyber wars' with anyone on FaceBook.** If someone is bothering you, simply block them. It isn't hard to do – and it's much more reasonable than throwing flames for the whole world to see.

Above all, use good common sense. Always think before you act – or before you hit a submit button. Consider your customers, your potential customers, business contacts, and potential business contacts – how will they view what you are about to do?

If you follow these no-no rules, you will almost always be just fine.

The FaceBook Frenzy: To Join or Not to Join?

No matter what type of application you are talking about in the online world, there will always be those who are all for it, and those who are against it. The same is true with FaceBook. There are those who claim that it is a waste of time, and others who are quickly building up their businesses – and their bottom lines – through this social networking site.

The fact is that if you become an active user of FaceBook, and you use the site in an acceptable, appropriate manner, it is far from a waste of time. It is a great way to connect with your customers on a more personal level, which helps to build greater trust and credibility with them. It is a fantastic way to generate new customers through building relationships with current customers and attracting the business of their friends.

FaceBook also allows you to connect more easily with potential joint venture partners. In fact, it gives you the opportunity to connect with people that you often wouldn't be able to connect with in other online venues. On top of this, it is an excellent way to work with your current joint venture partners as well.

You can notify potential customers and joint venture partners about upcoming product launches that you have, or that you are participating in – without spamming, by simply linking your twitter account to your profile or by using the 'what are you doing right now' feature on FaceBook.

FaceBook is especially valuable for Internet Marketers. In fact, as valuable as it once was – and still is – for college students, it is equally valuable for Internet Marketers, if not more so. The connections that can be made, and the relationships that can be built are more valuable than any other type of relationship building that you can do in the online world, and this includes other social networking sites.

www.ingramcontent.com/pod-product-compliance
Lightning Source LLC
LaVergne TN
LVHW020508080526
838202LV00057B/6247